DIANA BLOOMFIELD

THE ENGRAVER'S CUT

DIANA BLOOMFIELD

TWENTY-SIX WOOD ENGRAVINGS
CHOSEN BY THE ARTIST
WITH AN AUTOBIOGRAPHICAL
NOTE
AND BIBLIOGRAPHY

PRIMROSE HILL PRESS
OAK KNOLL PRESS

Published in 1998 by
Primrose Hill Press, 58 Carey St., London WC2A 2JB, UK
Oak Knoll Press, 414 Delaware St., New Castle, DE 19720, USA

© copyright Diana Bloomfield 1998

No part of this book may be reproduced in any form or
by any means without the prior permission in writing
from the publisher.

ISBN (UK): 1 90164 801 X
ISBN (USA): 1 884718 47 7

British Library Cataloguing-in-Publication Data.
A catalogue record for this book is available from
The British Library.

Library of Congress Cataloging-in-Publication Data
Bloomfield, Diana.
Diana Bloomfield: twenty-six wood engravings chosen by the
artist with an autobiographical note and bibliography.
48 p. 129x198 cm. -- (Engraver's cut series; no. 1)
Originally published: London: Primrose Academy, 1995.
ISBN 1-884718-47-7
1. Bloomfield, Diana -- Themes, motives. I. title. II. Series.
NE1147.6.B59B56   1998
769.92--DC21   97-43355
                                                          CIP

Engraver's Cut Series: No. 1

Based on the private press edition printed from the original blocks
by Sebastian Carter at The Rampant Lions Press for The Primrose
Academy, 1995, in a limited edition of 135 copies signed by the
artist. Copies of the limited edition are available from The Primrose
Academy, 20 Ainger Road, London NW3 3AS, England

All wood engravings are reproduced in their
original size
Cover design by Oblong
Printed in Great Britain by
Hobbs the Printers, Southampton

Contents

Autobiographical Note 1

Wood Engravings

from THE SILVER SWAN

Frog 7
Swans 7
Windmill 9
Fountain 9
Girl playing piano 11

from THE CRYSTAL CABINET

Rider on horse 11
Boys fishing on beach 13
Snake 13

from THE PERIODICAL

Swan and factory 15

for PENGUIN CLASSICS

Balzac 17
Alexander the Great 17
Piers Plowman 19

21 Lower Common South (letterhead) 19

from THE GREEN ROADS

Yarrow 21
Boy playing pipe 21
Daisies 23
Cow and cowherd 23
White horse on downs 25
Anemones 25

Salute the happy morn 27

Small chair 27

Telscombe Church 29

Rodmell Church.. 29

Archway 31

Eleanor Catherine James (bookplate) 31

Tribute to Lord Cobbold 33

Bibliography

Books Illustrated by Diana Bloomfield 35
Cover Designs for Oxford University Press .. 35
Penguin Classic Roundels 36
Bookplates 36
Letterheads.. 39
Books and Articles about or referring to
    Diana Bloomfield 40

Autobiographical Note

Poor health denied me all but minimal time at school. This gave me happy days of reading and drawing at home. When older, I went to the Harrow Art School, but art jobs then were difficult to find; so with financial trouble at home, I reluctantly agreed to take a job in the Bank of England. There, in spare time, I would write poems and make drawings for the Bank's magazine, *The Old Lady of Threadneedle Street*. I married in 1938, had three children, and lived near Hampstead Heath.

At the Hampstead Garden Suburb Institute I took classes in quill lettering under M. C. Oliver, pupil of Edward Johnston. This helped me to engrave letters later. Mr. Oliver was a hard taskmaster; never any praise and plenty of criticism! But he taught me how to cut quills for the smallest of letters. I wrote out poems; a book on my childhood on handmade paper, illustrated with linocuts, and a book I called *A Personal Alphabet*, an exercise for a combination of the foundational hand and Italian italics. All three were bound by my husband. I made maps of Oxford and Cambridge with facades of the college buildings, and one of Pembrokeshire, illustrated, with the Welsh names in blue and the English in black, and an heraldic shield that held a tame-looking bull!

I also took classes on textile design with Ronald Grierson, rug-designer. He had unusual teaching qualities: rather than telling me what I should do, he would display art magazines such as *Domus*, and the latest illustrated articles on Italian and Scandinavian furniture; I was settled on a long programme of designing textiles for that furniture. He also sent me to the British Museum for designs based on Mexican and African motifs, and to Kenwood, for my own 'Adam brothers' designs. I erred on being over-fussy, but Ronald, pencil poised, would bring the point down on my paper, and with this mark, would hold my wavering shapes together. Later I sold some of my designs to Liberty's and Heal's for manufacture.

About this time I was sent two old wood engraving tools, reputed to belong to the Dalziel brothers. I took one lesson from John Beedham on how to hold these tools before he became, alas, too ill to teach. I then decided to teach myself, engraving a number of the drawings in my sketch books, mainly of the activities on Hampstead Heath: little boys playing football, climbing trees and flying kites. This was a joyous phase of my life; walking alone, sketching, mainly with a pen, looking for suitable subjects that held black and white, but also the innumerable tones of grey, lovingly observed in the exquisite work of Thomas Bewick.

It was a lucky day when I dared to send some of these first efforts to Beatrice Warde, a highly regarded expert in typography. She was a remarkable woman and brilliant lecturer, with whom I was to become friends. We visited each other's homes. Observing my sketch books were full of country subjects, she suggested an outing together; she met me at Epsom, in high-heeled shoes. We drove in a hired chauffeur-driven car to some woods, and she said 'Now, Diana, show me Nature!'

But her kindness and encouragement for my work were generous. She introduced me to the Oxford University Press, Penguin Books, and several private presses. I started work engraving for the rejacketing of the Oxford Standard Authors and World Classics. For these I was working for John Bell, whose sympathetic nature turned the jobs into a joy: 'What do you think of, Diana, when I say "Keats's letters"?' I replied: 'I think of Keats's house in Hampstead where he wrote most of them'. 'Good,' said he. 'Then go and draw it'. During that exciting time I engraved roundels for Penguin Classics. These jobs filled some of the gaps in my education. I engraved Alexander the Great, studying coins in the British Museum; Goethe, as a dignified old man; Balzac, with his fleshy, powerful face and shoulders, and among others, 'Piers Plowman', quite a tricky one with a Christ-like figure wielding a fourteenth-century plough while a monk lies in a ditch in the foreground. All in a one-and-a-quarter inch circle!

The first book I illustrated was *A Puffin Quartet of Poets* for Penguin Books. The first of the poets was Eleanor Farjeon, that author of charming stories for children. She asked me to engrave Timothy riding a weasel from England to Spain. I surrounded myself with my father's old animal books, gave Timothy a whip, and drew his mother in an apron, running out of her cottage. James Reeves, the second poet, wanted a snail eating ivy. E.V. Rieu, the brilliant translator of classics, a unicorn gazing into a tropical stream and saying 'What a beautiful creature I am!' while six flamingoes flew overhead. Lastly, Ian Seraillier, for whom I engraved the Kon Tiki raft! It was a big challenge, but one I wanted to rise to, to be happy with it myself, and to please Hans Schmoller, then director of Penguin Books, for whom I was rather fearfully working, and for whom I had a great respect.

In the lettering world I knew I could do no better than study the beautiful work of Reynolds Stone. My earliest attempts were very clumsy, but I found as I had more commissions for bookplates and letter-headings, confidence grew, and I was able to get into a state of happy rhythm as I engraved. I had the job of designing and engraving about thirty labels for Vista Books, 'Pocket Poets'. I had been asked to enhance the names of the poets with a minimum of flourishes. This helped me to control the designs and keep them in sober taste.

I am not in sympathy with mermaids as subjects for bookplates. It could have been laughable when Beatrice Warde asked me to do two mermaids swimming in opposite directions, across the sea, holding books - for Ambassador Books,

Books Across the Sea. I engraved the mermaids holding the books above the waves, high and dry. But it was really a subject for Eric Ravilious, whose engravings could give anything charm and a sense of reality in a few areas of tool-mark pattern.

Whenever I received commissions for a bookplate or letterheading, I would eagerly look at the words to visualise what shape they would best fit; then what letters to use whose ascenders or descenders suggested a flourish that enhanced the design without spoiling readability. I would then write the words, generally in Italian italics and trace them backwards onto the wood. I learnt that it was important to engrave each part of a letter with one cut typical of the tool, so that serifs, for example, should be expressed with one push of the graver. A small mistake was better left; no fussing improved it. A larger one, and I had to begin again with a fresh block.

My work for publishers in New York included, for Holt, Rinehart and Winston, *The Green Roads*, *The Crystal Cabinet* and *The Silver Swan*; and for Thomas Crowell and Company, *Wordsworth*. My favourite is *The Green Roads* with poems by Edward Thomas, who also loved the simple things in the country - anemones, yarrow and daisies; and light flooding across an early morning scene, as I have tried to show in the cowherd and cows. I loved drawing domestic subjects; flowerpots, watering cans, and even a fork stuck in a compost heap!

Although I no longer engrave, I teach wood-engraving to a group of students in my home town of Lewes. They are most of them dear friends who have been in my class for many years. I love to see them bowed over their work, dedicated to these steel tools and small blocks of wood. I will often start them with engraving a pattern to show what the tip of each tool can produce. Sketch books are encouraged, and most of them are soon launched into engraving our local buildings and the surrounding Downs.

A few whom I taught in the City Literary Institute a quarter of a century ago continue to send me their prints, which fills me with a sense of working with them still.

Frog from THE SILVER SWAN

Swans from THE SILVER SWAN

Windmill from THE SILVER SWAN

Fountain from THE SILVER SWAN

Girl playing piano from THE SILVER SWAN

Rider on horse from THE CRYSTAL CABINET

Boys fishing on beach from THE CRYSTAL CABINET

Snake from THE CRYSTAL CABINET

Swan and factory from THE PERIODICAL

Balzac for PENGUIN CLASSICS

Alexander the Great for PENGUIN CLASSICS

Piers Plowman for PENGUIN CLASSICS

21 Lower Common South (letterhead)

Yarrow from THE GREEN ROADS

Boy playing pipe from THE GREEN ROADS

Daisies from THE GREEN ROADS

Cow and cowherd from THE GREEN ROADS

White horse on downs from THE GREEN ROADS

Anemones from THE GREEN ROADS

Salute the happy morn

Small chair

Telscombe Church

Rodmell Church

Archway

Eleanor Catherine James (bookplate)

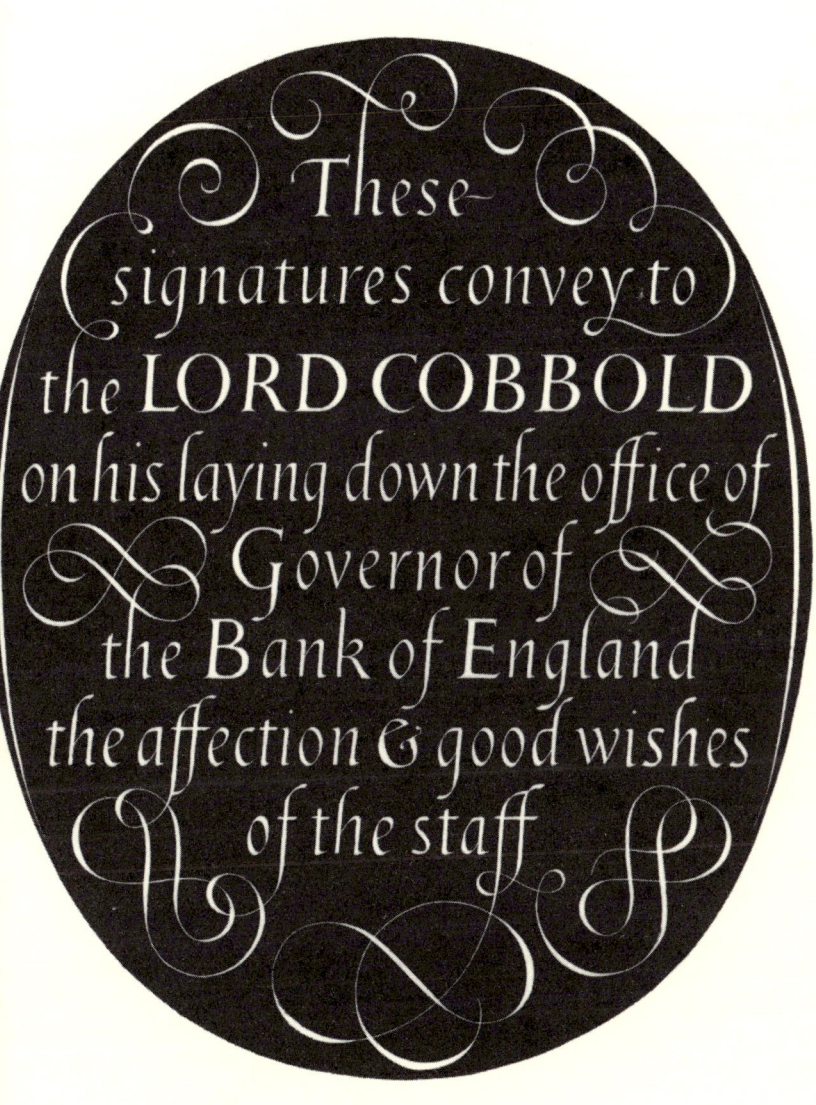

Tribute to Lord Cobbold

Books Illustrated by Diana Bloomfield

A Puffin Quartet of Poets, ed. by Eleanor Graham 1958
Come Hither, Walter de la Mare, Constable & Company Ltd., London 1960
The Crystal Cabinet: An invitation to poetry chosen by Horace Gregory and Maria Laturenska, 1962
The Man's Book, Eyre & Spottiswoode
Twenty-Five Poems by Evelyn Ansell, The Vine Press, Hemingford Grey, Cambridge, 1963
Poems of William Wordsworth selected by Elinor Parker, Thomas & Crowell Company, N.Y., 1964
The Green Roads, Poems by Edward Thomas chosen and with an introduction by Eleanor Farjeon, 1965
The Silver Swan, Holt Rinehart & Winston
The Palaces of Europe, (pen drawings) Weidenfeld & Nicholson

Cover Designs for Oxford University Press

World Classics
Poems of Robert Herrick
Poems of Samuel Taylor Coleridge
The Origin of Species Charles Darwin
Aeneid, Georgics and Ecolgues, Virgil
Letters of John Keats
Life of Charlotte Bronte

Standard Authors
The Poems of John Keats
Poetical Works, Wordsworth
The Poems of William Cowper
The Poems of John Dryden
The Poems of Gray and Collins
The Poems of Sir Walter Scott
Boswell and Johnson
Arthur Hugh Clough

and 30 "The Pocket Poets", Edward Hulton

Penguin Classic Roundels

Balzac, Domestic Peace & other stories
The Cloud of Unknowing
Goethe's Faust II
Gogol's "Dead Souls"
Alexander the Great (Arrians Life of)
Stendhal, The Charterhouse of Parma
Langland's Piers Plowman

Bookplates

1953/4
Philip Beddingham
Diana Bloomfield
Julia Mary Bloomfield
J.M.B (Julia Mary Bloomfield)

Kenneth Bloomfield
Kenneth Bloomfield
Y.K.B. (Kenneth Bloomfield)
Ex Libris Martin Bloomfield
Sarah Bloomfield
Sarah Caroline Emily Bloomfield
Ex Gillian Brandes Libris
Wallace Breem Ex Libris
Ruth Halliday
Leslie Kenneth O'Brien

1955
D.B. (Diana Bloomfield)
The Hall N.W.3 Ex Libris
Olive May McQuillan
The Monotype School, Students Library
The Mount Girls Preparatory School
Sydney Patrick Rose
Ruth Williams
Ruth Williams

1956
Arthur Giardelli. An Ambassador Book. Books across the Sea
Ex Beatrice Warde Libris
H. J. Willis
Eleanor James
Michael O'Brien

1958
Leon Bagrit

H. H. Willis

1959
This book belongs to the Ceylon Tea Centre
John Murray Coates
Phyllis and Annesley Voysey

1960
Richard Hall

1961
Kenneth Cross
Andrew Harvey
Dorothy Thornycroft

1962
Joan Farjeon
Elizabeth Voysey
Elizabeth Voysey
Ex libris John Voysey

1963
Diana Bloomfield
Eleanor Catherine James
Michael John O'Brien
Judith Harries Williams
Carol Anne Young

1965
Philip Beddingham
Kenneth Bloomfield

Pamela Lister
Ernest Percival Pearce
Georgina Rowlatt

1966
Marilyn Sjoberg

1967
Daniel Pedoe

1968
Michael Estorick

1970
The Bookplate Society
Kenneth Guichard
The Dean and Chapters Library Norwich

1972
Ex Libris Brian Runnett

Date unknown
Denise & Car Cowles-Voysey

Letterheads

Raymond Lister
Hans Schmoller
Edmund Penning-Rowsell
Beatrice Warde

Constable Books for Boys and Girls
The Golden Head Press (Cambridge)
"The Old Lady of Threadneedle Street" (Bank of England magazine)
Sir David Goldberg
- and many more including family

Books and Articles about or referring to Diana Bloomfield

"The Old Lady" article by John Newson (Bank of England magazine, 1965)

"Profile of an Artist" by Brian North Lee (The Bookplate Journal)

Matrix 13, 14 and 16, John Randle

"A Fearful Joy" Diana Bloomfield (the Private Library, Spring 1974)

"Diana Bloomfield: A Tribute" Edward Burrett (Penmiel Press)

"The Bookplates of Diana Bloomfield" by Philip Beddingham (American Society of Bookplate Collectors and Designers 1969/70)

Based on the private press edition printed from the original
blocks by Sebastian Carter at The Rampant Lions Press for
The Primrose Academy, 1995,
in a limited edition of 135 copies signed by the artist.
Copies of the limited edition are available from
The Primrose Academy, 20 Ainger Road,
London NW3 3AS, England